THE REMARKABLE LIFE OF CHET ENSTROM,
HIS ALMOND TOFFEE, AND A FAMILY LEGACY

THE REMARKABLE LIFE OF CHET ENSTROM,
HIS ALMOND TOFFEE, AND A FAMILY LEGACY

LEGENDS OF THE GRAND VALLEY
GRAND JUNCTION, COLORADO 2014

Library of Congress Cataloging in Publication Data

Ann Enstrom Scott
Ken Johnson
Chet. The remarkable life of Chet Enstrom, his almond toffee and a family legacy

ISBN 978-0-692-28640-1

THIS BOOK WAS DESIGNED AND PRODUCED BY
Grand Valley Magazine, Inc.
PO Box 2509
Grand Junction, CO 81502
Kitty Nicholason, Designer

PRINTED BY
CPC Solutions
2800 Printers Way
Grand Junction, CO 81506

Historic Story Sculptures

Dalton Trumbo

George A. Crawford

Walter Walker & Pres Walker

Sister Mary Balbina Farrell

William Moyer

John Otto

Operation Foresight

Prinster Brothers

Chet & Vernie Enstrom

Story Sculpture Companion Books

Eclipse by Dalton Trumbo, reprinted 2006

John Otto & The Colorado National Monument

Operation Foresight: 50 Years

City Market and the Brothers Four

Chet: The Remarkable Life of Chet Enstrom, his Almond Toffee and a Family Legacy

CONTENTS

The Legacy

ANN ENSTROM SCOTT WROTE THE VARIOUS chapters in this book over several years, just to share family memories and stories of her parents with her children and grandchildren. They chronicle the lives of those parents, Chet and Vernie Enstrom, and the fascinating history of two family businesses, both successful and both memorable. They're full of delicious tidbits of happenings through the years plus a continuing story; how three generations of the Enstrom family has quietly built a world-famous business.

Ann's gift of her memories to those children and grandchildren capture poignant and fascinating details of how Chet and Vernie first built an award-winning ice cream business and then launched what has become today's Enstrom Candies.

That alone is amazing 85 years later, but both Chet and Vernie were also community leaders, helping build the foundation of our community.

It was ice cream for the first 31 years, and then Ann tells how they built her dad's "hobby," making candy, into a bigger business.

Chet and Vernie didn't know whether it would succeed or not but that didn't matter. After all, it was just going to be a part-time, mom and pop project. Something to keep them busy.

Their story is about imagination, hard work, family, and giving back to the community. It details the changing times from the early days of automobiles to the space age, and how Grand Junction's

Chet — Mr. Almond Toffee

most unusual business, this legacy candy company, grew. It's a continuing story, too; how three generations of the family has built a world-famous business and a fourth generation is poised to carry on.

Ann tells about their start-up dairy business, specializing in ice cream, and how her dad's making a bit of Christmas candies for family and friends made new friends world wide.

That original dairy business brought young Chet and Vernie with their two kids, Emil and Ann, to Grand Junction in 1929. The timing might have been a bit better because in just six months the stock market crashed and the Great Depression was underway.

Regardless, Chet and his partner, Harry Jones, never missed a payroll as they nurtured their Velvet Ice Cream until it was the dominant regional brand. They arranged to have Jones sell his half

The new candy factory on the left,
Velvet Ice Cream on the right, November 1962

Emil and Chet pour a mix for candy canes onto the cooling table.

of the company to Vernie in 1958 and retire to California. The company was 29 years old.

The part-time candy business had a few customers, plus Chet was donating candy to various good causes every year, including the annual Lions Club Carnival. Even when it was being made in the basement of their home it was obvious that Chet was a master candy maker. Family and friends got a lot of candy through the years. Early customers were friends and business acquaintances who had learned of its Christmas availability.

In 1960 they sold the ice cream business, now beset with demands for low-fat ice cream that Chet detested, to Clymer's Rose Glen Dairy. That let the Enstroms give the candy business a try.

In 1962 they tore down the house on the north side of the Velvet plant and opened a brand new candy factory there at 212 S. Seventh Street. When the Clymer family moved their ice cream operation out of the Velvet plant in 1965, that space also became part of their growing candy world. Enstrom Candy Co. then totaled about 7,500 square feet. That year Chet and Vernie had seen their "little mom and pop business" produce about 20,000 pounds of toffee.

The second Enstrom generation arrived in 1966, when Chet became a Colorado State Senator. Their son Emil had an Iowa State University degree in dairy management and was a dairyman in his own right, working for Beatrice Foods before coming back to town to join the candy company.

The business steadily grew and Emil and his wife Mary bought the family business in 1970. One of their sons, Rick (who, following

Three generations of a family business in front of the original Candy Kitchen in 1989: Vernie, Chet, Mary, Emil, Jamee, Doug

in Granddad's political footprints, had been a Mesa County Commissioner) opened a Denver Enstrom's store in 1986.

In 1979 the third generation arrived; Emil and Mary's daughter and her husband, Jamee and Doug Simons, joined the business. Ten years later Enstrom Candies expanded into a new 20,000-square-foot building. Doug Simons was now president. The new space was overdue; in 1988, Enstroms produced 360,000 pounds of Almond Toffee. The mailing had grown to over 50,000 names!

Emil and Mary's hard work and innovations had paid off with solid growth, and in 1993 they sold the business to Doug and Jamee. Mary died in August that year and Emil continued to help guide the company until his death in January 1998.

In 2002 the building was expanded further into today's plant. The Simons continue the business and two sons are now involved. Doug Jr. is 30 and Jim is 28. Growth has been a constant and, once again, the building is too small.

Thanks to Ann's stories, we get a warmly fascinating look into the happenings through the years that led to Almond Toffee by Chet and the successful and unusual family business.

How unusual? By 2010, the 50th anniversary of Enstrom Candies, they shipped over 700,000 pounds of that World Famous Almond Toffee. The company keeps growing and expanding with multiple stores and a huge mailing list of customers. Today boxes of that toffee go worldwide.

That hard-working first generation built an amazing foundation. Each following generation then built its own dynamic legacy — success building on success.

And coming full circle, today they offer dozens of other hand-made candies and even some ice cream, harkening back to those 1929 roots when Chet and his partner, Harry Jones, made Velvet Ice Cream.

And when Chet Enstrom, stirring the freshest ingredients with a wooden paddle in a copper pot, used skill and loving care to make a little candy for friends and family at Christmas.

— KEN JOHNSON

Jones-Enstrom Ice Cream Company

"Dad was very pleased when he developed a sugar-free ice cream that was pretty good for those who were diabetic. Diabetic people really appreciated it."
— ANN ENSTROM SCOTT

THE JONES-ENSTROM ICE CREAM COMPANY opened for business in Grand Junction on March 4, 1929. In the fall of 1928, Mr. Harry Jones asked Dad if he would like to go into partnership with him and buy a dairy someplace. Dad realized that this was a real opportunity for him; Mother reluctantly went along with the idea. I was three years old and Emil was nine months old at the time. It was very hard for her to leave family and friends and her new home, which Dad had just built for her, and move to an unknown area.

Mr. Jones had been a dairy traveling salesman from Larkspur and he had been calling regularly on Barthel's Confectionery, where Dad had been working for several years. He liked Dad's work ethic and the wonderful ice cream he was making. Mr. Jones knew there were a few dairies for sale in Colorado and New Mexico. He and Dad discussed which ones would offer the most opportunities and they decided on Grand Junction, Colorado. Oil Shale development was **just around the corner** and Grand Junction would become a "boom **town." As we all know, that** "corner" was very long and instead of **a boom, the Great Depression started** the following October and **the banks closed a few months later. However,** the Joneses and the

Enstroms were never disappointed that they had chosen Grand Junction as the place to go into business and to raise their families. They all thought Grand Junction was the greatest.

Dad and Mr. Jones, along with a very few employees, made the products. They then sold them in the retail area of the building. When Mr. Jones could get away, he would call on grocery stores, drug stores, and any place where they might sell ice cream to see if he could get their business. The company owned two Model A Ford Coupes. Dad removed the rumble seats and replaced them with wooden "truck beds" so they could deliver ice cream to their customers. The trucks were painted bright yellow with red lettering on the side so they were quite visible.

The Jones-Enstrom Ice Cream Company
on South Seventh Street in 1929

The renovated and updated Velvet Ice Cream plant, circa early 1930s

The ice cream they delivered was frozen in 10-gallon cans. Each can was put into a heavily insulated "jacket" and then a lot of ice was put between the can and the jacket. Ice cream was prepared the same way when it went to customers by railroad. When dry ice became available, it truly simplified the process.

The business grew at a pretty good pace considering how little money was available for luxuries. Even five cents for an ice cream cone was hard to come by. Because the dairy was close to the railroad station, many homeless people (mostly men) would walk by the

A Velvet Ice Cream ad
in *The Daily Sentinel*

dairy and stop and ask for something to eat. Dad couldn't afford to give them all ice cream but he always gave them milk.

There were always eight to ten flavors of ice cream and two or three flavored sherbets for sale in the retail store. Each month there was a special flavor. Dad was always willing to try something new.

One time he and Mother were on a champagne flight going to a meeting some place and for dessert they were served champagne sherbet. It was really good, so when Dad got home, he went right to work to figure out how to make a champagne sherbet. It became a popular special.

Some of the deliciously unusual Velvet flavors were Peppermint Stick, Butter Brickle, and Tutti-Fruti.

Dad was very pleased when he developed a sugar-free ice cream that was pretty good for those who were diabetic. Diabetic people really appreciated it.

They sold not only ice cream at Jones-Enstrom Ice Cream Company, but they also sold butter, eggs, fresh cottage cheese, and ice cream novelties. Dad also made a fresh fruit punch which was very popular. For years it was served at all of the school proms in the area and it was served for many special occasions. Dad made beautiful mints for special occasions long before he was in the candy business. If someone wanted a different treat for a special occasion, Dad could decorate slices of ice cream with something appropriate for the occasion, or he could make something quite special out of the many ice cream molds he had, or he could decorate a delicious ice cream cake.

After the war, the business grew rapidly. Refrigeration was very much improved so the ice cream was shipped to many places in western Colorado and eastern Utah.

Dad was active in the Colorado Dairy Association, serving as president for two years. For several years there was a competition held at the annual Colorado Dairy Association meeting in Denver to see which ice cream was rated the highest. For years Dolly Madison from Denver would beat Velvet Ice Cream by just a point or two. Finally, Grand Junction's Velvet Ice Cream was Number 1. What a special occasion that was!

The Palisade Drug
Company building
had a Velvet Ice
Cream sign painted
on the highway side.

Vernie and Chet stand next to the Fruita Ice Cream Parlor in 1986. The sign painted on the side of the building was a constant reminder to ask for Velvet Ice Cream.

Dad was also active in the International Ice Cream Association which I am sure is what encouraged President Eisenhower to select Dad as one of the five dairymen to represent the United States at the World Dairy Congress in Italy in 1956. This was a great experience for Dad.

Mr. Jones wanted to retire in 1958. They worked out a plan so Vernie could buy his share and Mr. Jones moved to California. Chet and Vernie continued to run the business from then on.

People started wanting a fat-free ice cream. Dad just couldn't make a poor grade of ice cream, which is what he thought a low-fat ice cream was. He sold the Velvet Ice Cream Company to Clymer's Rose Glen Dairy in 1960 and turned his full attention to making great candy.

Backstory Notes

One of the clever ways Jones and Enstrom kept their Velvet Ice Cream in public view was with signs on various customer buildings. A delightful example is the Palisade Drug Company building, right on Palisade's Main Street and East Third Street corner, when Third St. was also Highways 6 & 24. It's like a Velvet bookend when paired with a similar one in Fruita.

It would have been hard to miss that painted Velvet Ice Cream sign on the side of the building!

Priscilla Walker of the Palisade Historical Society has some detail about the building and says their "walking tour" information is: "The brick–block building was built in 1905 by James Purcell. The Palisade Drug Company occupied this corner space from 1920 until 1998, featuring a popular soda fountain."

She has other history too.

It turns out Purcell built it for a special use. From 1905 through 1908 it was the "Brown Palace" bar, said to have been named for Purcell's bartender Robert S. Brown. Palisade voted "dry" in 1908 and that was the end of Purcell's bar. He also was a Coors distributor and made beer in his building. In 1912 it became a grocery and meat shop. That continued until the Palisade Drug took over.

It's possible that it was a pool hall and cigar shop for a while. That would have followed his business trail in Grand Junction, where he opened his first saloon in 1891. He owned the Senate in Grand Junction in 1895 and ran it until his death in 1935. Grand Junction voted dry a year after Palisade and Purcell's long-running success with his two Grand Junction saloons, the Senate and the Annex, (where he also made Coors beer) also ended. The Senate became a cigar store and billiard hall that lasted until 1955.

Like the Palisade Drug building, the old Senate building still stands. It is now a fly-fishing shop. In Palisade the old Purcell Building is for sale and the Velvet Ice Cream sign is gone.

Beautifully decorated all-chocolate specials

Growing Up
Chester Kermit Enstrom

*"The teachers were barely out of high school and the big boys
gave them so much trouble the short time that they were in
school that it was hard to keep teachers."*
— CHET ENSTROM

MY FATHER OFTEN TOLD ME THAT ONE OF HIS earliest memories took place when he was very young. His grandparents had come to visit for the day and, being good Swedes and generous people, they had brought a special gift — a large hunk of fresh Limburger cheese. When his grandparents left, Dad started to cry profusely. When his mother asked him what was making him cry, he answered, "They left that stinky cheese here." If you have ever smelled fresh Limburger cheese, you will understand his tears. Dad decided then he would never eat cheese.

When he was in the ice cream business, he made a lot of cottage cheese, which he would taste to see if it was right, then he would spit it out. He didn't knowingly ever eat cheese of any kind until quite late in life when he eventually discovered that cottage cheese covered with a lot of fruit wasn't too bad.

Dad was born in Woodhull, Illinois on November 27, 1902. His parents had both come from Sweden with their parents. Both families ended up living near Galesburg, Illinois. Gustaf Emil Enstrom and Emma Cristina Anderson were married there in 1901. I am not sure what my grandfather Enstrom did for a living after

Young Chet, on the farm

they were first married but he soon tried farming in Iowa. It was in Iowa where my father started to school in a one-room country schoolhouse about one-and-a-quarter mile away. Of course he had to walk to school and take his lunch. The following is what he told me about the country school:

> "Since we lived in a Swedish settlement, most of the students were Swedes. There were a lot of boys 19 or 20 years old in the lower grades because they could only go to school for a few

winter months when the snow was so deep they couldn't work in the fields. So we kids learned a lot from them (and some things we didn't need to know quite so soon). The teachers were barely out of high school and the big boys gave them so much trouble the short time that they were in school that it was hard to keep teachers. The boys would do such things as chase the teacher's horse away, mess with the wood-burning stove so the fire would go out, and other unkind things. But I learned a lot and was ahead of the students when we moved back to Illinois."

My grandfather learned after a few years that farming was not his "thing" so they moved to Galesburg where he went to work for the DeLaval Separator Company, a company which made equipment to separate cream from the milk so people could make cheese, ice cream, and so on. He was very good at sales so the company moved him several times and Dad ended up going to several grade schools. They moved back to Galesburg when my grandfather contracted tuberculosis. He was in and out of the hospital and finally the family was told that his only hope was to move to Colorado.

It was very hard for the family (which by then included my father's sisters, Frances and Kathryn) to leave their extended family and friends to go where they knew no one or what to expect. They moved to Colorado Springs because they had an acquaintance who could help them find a house to rent. Grandfather was so sick by the time they got to Colorado Springs that my grandmother wouldn't leave him, so Dad had to assume a lot of responsibility. He was 13, Frances was 11-and-a-half, and Kathryn was eight. Dad found the school where they belonged and took his sisters and enrolled them all in their proper grades. After one year Dad had to stay out of school and work to help support the family.

By the time my grandfather died, less than two years after moving to Colorado Springs, the family was out of money and the rent was due. Dad had to find money for the rent. He had heard that a neighbor was a Mason and that Masons helped people, so Dad went to see the gentleman and explained the circumstances. He promised to pay back a certain amount each week out of his pay.

Kathryn, eight, and Chet, 13, at home
at 640 Willamette, Colorado Springs
during World War I

The nice man loaned Dad the money and Dad was always so proud of the fact that he never missed a week paying the man back the promised amount.

Even though Grandfather's death was a tragedy, it was easier for the family to survive after his death. Grandmother went to work selling goods in a bakery and later worked for a very fine dry cleaner doing the hardest pressing jobs. I remember going to see her at work many years later, when I was a little girl, and perspiration was rolling down her face. There was no air conditioning and she was still pressing tiny pleats in fancy dresses for the ladies who lived by the Broadmoor Hotel.

While in high school, Dad worked for the newspaper publisher, taking papers off the press at 2:30 in the morning. He then carried a paper route about 15 miles throughout the Ivywild and Broadmoor Districts in Colorado Springs. He was a good student so he was able to work the long hours and still go to school. In the summertime when school was out he also worked in an ice cream plant.

He often told me that his favorite teacher was an English teacher who helped him get rid of his Swedish accent. Then in his senior year, about the first of March, the house the family was renting was sold so Dad had to take two days off to find a house that they could afford to rent. When he went back to school and told the principal what had happened, the principal thought he was a part of a bunch of seniors who had been giving the school trouble with truancy and so he was expelled along with them. About 10 days later he got a letter from the school saying they had made a terrible mistake and for him to get back in school. By then my Dad had a job making $16 a week so he didn't go back to school and didn't get to graduate.

He did finally get a high school diploma in 1970 when he was Chairman of the Education Committee in the State Senate.

When the Superintendent of Schools in Colorado Springs found out what had happened to Dad so many years earlier he had Palmer High School include Dad in the graduating class of 1970. Since Dad was Chairman of the Education Committee it was thought that he should have a high school diploma. Dad was very pleased to finally have a high school diploma.

Chet, baby Katherine, and Frances

Dad always loved sports. In high school he somehow managed to play enough tennis to win a nice tennis racket. He kept it for many years and he taught me to play tennis with it. He also played baseball, which was one of his favorite sports.

When Dad was working in the ice cream plant during the summer, his job was to deliver ice cream on his bicycle (I don't know how he kept it from melting). Because of Dad's eagerness to please his boss, his boss took a special interest in him and would occasionally take Dad along to deliver large ice cream orders or would take him to the bank with him. His boss sometimes just carried his deposit in his hat or sometimes he used a moneybag. This really impressed Dad and he decided then that someday he was going to be in business and carry money to the bank in a bag.

The job Dad got when he quit high school was at Barthel's Confectionery. That was where he learned both the ice cream and the candy business. He worked there for nine years, steadily trying to improve Barthel's ice cream. He even paid his own way to go to Iowa State University on two occasions for two-week courses in ice cream making. He improved the ice cream a great deal during this time. He made a much richer and smoother ice cream than anyone else, which people loved.

He learned the candy business by spying on the candy maker at Barthel's. In the winter the ice cream business slowed down and Dad had time to watch the candy maker and learn the trade. In those days recipes were not published. Candy makers developed their own recipes and they didn't share them. The candy maker let Dad wash the pots and kettles. While Dad was washing pots, he watched what the candy maker was doing and would write it down. He had very good eyes and could see when the candy maker weighed an amount of an ingredient and he also watched the cooking thermometer.

Dad had learned enough that when the candy maker decided to open his own candy store in west Colorado Springs, Dad told Mr. Barthel that he thought he could handle making candy along with the ice cream. Mr. Barthel was a fine candy maker himself, so with his help Dad became a "Candy Man." He made all kinds of candy:

caramels, Christmas candy canes, hard candies, and chocolates of all kinds.

Midway through his career with Barthel's, Dad had become good friends with a boy named Boss Berry. Boss lived across the street from a girl named Helen and Helen's best friend was Vernie Morgan. The four of them became friends and one day Boss suggested that he and Dad take the girls to the movie. Dad thought that would be a good idea but he wanted to take the one with the pretty brown eyes. That was Vernie. Apparently that was okay with Boss because a couple of years later, May 21, 1924, Chet and Vernie were married at Castle Rock.

Those nine years at Barthel's had prepared Dad well to take the opportunity to go to Grand Junction with his partner, Harry Jones, and start their own business.

The Candy Man

*"Raquel Welch ordered some candy, the boys helping
Dad wanted to deliver it in person.
Someone ordered a box sent to John Wayne."*
— ANN ENSTROM SCOTT

A COUPLE OF YEARS BEFORE MOTHER DIED, THERE was an article in the *Denver Post* telling about the success of Enstroms Almond Toffee. I took the article over to share with Mother at the Atrium. She read the article and said, "When I married your Dad, I never expected the name "Enstrom" to become famous." I don't know how well-known something has to be to become famous, but Enstrom's Almond Toffee is certainly well known around the state of Colorado and far beyond.

It was never Dad's goal to be famous or wealthy. As the toffee business grew, he would always express his amazement at how many people ordered toffee at Christmastime. Dad's goal in life was to do the very best he could in everything he did, no matter how menial or how important the job was, to help his fellow man when he could, and to find happiness along the way. I can truly say that I think he achieved his goal.

I researched "toffee" on the Internet but could not find much about it except that in England in the 1850s some were making a candy called taffie or toffee. While it had butter, sugar, and nuts, it didn't sound much like the toffee that Dad made. It did show a similar delicacy has been around for about 175 years. Our family moved to Grand Junction from Colorado Springs so that Dad and

Reddi-Whip hostesses concoct dessert for the officers and 500 delegates at the Western States Diary Association convention. Chet is president.

Harry Jones could be partners in the Jones-Enstrom Ice Cream Company. The new ice cream company opened March 4, 1929 and the Great Depression started in October. The banks closed a few months later. It was very rough going but Dad and Harry were very proud that they did not lay anyone off and never missed a payday for their employees. During this time and for several years the production of candy was not even a thought.

Dad was a master of both candy and ice cream when he left Colorado Springs. About 1934 he was making some candies again,

Chet and Vernie work with Shirley Gibson
as they make some specialty candies.

A gallon can of almonds is the final addition to the hot mix. (Photo by Bob Grant, *Daily Sentinel*)

now in our kitchen using Mom's stove. Caramels in particular would pop and splatter on the walls and floor, which didn't make Mom happy. When he finally had the time and a little money ahead, he set up a primitive candy-making operation in our basement at 1250 Grand Avenue.

Chet and Vernie dump the 28
pounds of hot almond toffee mix
onto the cooling table. (Photo by
Bob Grant, *Daily Sentinel*)

Even though the conditions in the basement were cramped
(and truly inadequate) Dad was able to make chocolate and vanilla
caramels, and he dipped caramels, cherries and various cream
centers in milk chocolate. He did a beautiful job of dipping. Later
he expanded to fudge, divinity, and nut clusters. He did not make
candy to sell. He made it only to give away. And he made it only
at Christmastime, when the ice cream business slowed down. He
gave boxes of candy to friends, salesmen who called on the dairy,
and dairymen from the Collbran and Mesa area from whom he
bought cream for the ice cream. My brother Emil and I each took a
Christmas box to our teachers.

Chet pours a coating of chocolate over the cooling toffee. (Photo by Bob Grant, *Daily Sentinel*)

During WWII when sugar was rationed Dad offered to make any kind of candy for parents to send to the boys in the service. The parents had to furnish sugar and he would furnish the rest of the ingredients. He would make whatever kind of candy that would ship and keep the best for the location where the recipient was located. Word was getting out about Dad's candy and the response was favorable.

Lions Club members, meeting weekly at the LaCourt Hotel, would empty the sugar bowls into napkins and give the sugar to Dad so he could keep making peanut brittle and other candy for the yearly Carnivals.

Chet flips a 14-pound toffee square so crushed almonds can cover both sides.
(Photo by Bob Grant, *Daily Sentinel*)

A smiling Chet scatters the finishing
touch of crushed almonds over the
new chocolate-covered batch. (Photo
by Bob Grant, *Daily Sentinel*)

Every month Dad or Harry would come up with an idea for a special ice cream flavor to be the special of the month. They were running out of ideas when Dad remembered about some candy and a recipe a Greek salesman had given him while he was still in Colorado Springs. It was called toffee. The salesman said that it was made of butter, sugar, and nuts, which wasn't much help, but his recipe also included stirring the mix with a wooden paddle and cooling it on marble.

Dad decided to see if he could come up with something they could chop up and put in vanilla ice cream. It took a lot of experimenting because the heat and the butter and other ingredients all have to be exact or the candy is a flop.

It was Mother's job to take a long-handled spoon and dip it into the boiling candy and pull out a nut. She would quickly douse the nut in cold water then bite into the nut to see if it was cooked. Not a very scientific method. If the nut was done, then the folks had to quickly pour the candy onto a water-cooled table. Finally Dad hit on something that was close to the candy the salesman had given him. They chopped it up and put it in vanilla ice cream they named "Butter Brickle."

It was a hit! It became a special flavor quite often. Dad kept working on the recipe to see if he could come up with something that could be a confection rather than just something to cut up and put in ice cream. During the late 50s and early 60s, Dad was on the Governing Board of Colorado State University. He would take toffee to the meetings and everyone who got some of the candy raved about it. Dad consulted with the food scientists at CSU and they gave him some additional ideas, some of which worked and some that didn't. Mostly, he needed help on how to extend the shelf life of the toffee. They did suggest that he pack the candy in dark paper.

Also during the early 1940s Dad was appointed to the board of directors of the International Association of Ice Cream Manufacturers, with members from England, France, Canada, and the United States. Dad would take toffee to the meetings. The members loved the candy and suggested that he go into the toffee-producing business. So he sent letters to all the members of the association and asked them to send his toffee as gifts. It became internationally popular from the beginning.

By 1954 the candy business grew to the point it needed its own space. They rented a place from Charlie Mars across the alley from the Velvet plant for the first real candy kitchen. The business grew further, and by Christmas 1959 about 4,000 pounds of almond toffee was made. Orders went to three-fourths of the United States and to France, Germany, Iran, and Japan.

In 1962 the business was in a brand new plant, at 212 S. Seventh St. on the north side of the Velvet building. The sign said "Enstrom Candy Company." Also on the face of the new building was a significant saying: "Almond Toffee by Chet."

The original idea after they sold the ice cream business in 1960 was that Dad and Mother would work together making toffee in the winter and they would play golf and fish during the rest of the year. It was to be just a "mom and pop" operation but it grew faster than they ever dreamed it would. Dad taught some of his workers how to dip chocolates and soon there was a variety of candy available. In 1965 they expanded into the Velvet building.

At Easter the store was filled with decorated, hand-dipped candy Easter eggs. At Christmas Dad made beautiful candy canes along with other special Christmas candies. A Christmas letter along with an order blank was mailed to all previous customers and the mail order list grew fast. Mother continued to work along with Dad.

It was still a "mom and pop" operation with a little extra help at Christmas and Easter but it was quickly growing into a full-time business. By 1966 the business had customers in all 50 states and 24 foreign countries.

It was in the spring of 1966 that Dad was appointed to fill the State Senate seat of Senator Ed Lamb. Dad had always wanted to do something politically to help his community and state. So he accepted the appointment. Dad felt that the toffee business was on its feet enough to support a family so he asked my brother Emil if he would like to try and make a go of it. Dad knew he could not run a candy business and do a good job as a State Senator. He preferred

being a Senator and Emil accepted the challenge. Emil quickly learned the candy business and he and his wife, Mary, brought new ideas and innovations that rapidly paid off. They truly made a success of the "mom and pop" business and bought it in 1970.

Their first almond toffee box was stylish. A red band with a "CKE" emblem on it encircled the one-pound box. The label read "Almond Toffee by Chet." Ingredients were "Grade A Creamery Butter, Sugar, Almonds and Milk Chocolate." And it publicized Grand Junction, Colorado.

The Christmas mailing list started reflecting that the toffee was on its way to becoming recognized all over the world. People ordered from everywhere. The editor of the *New York Times* ordered three boxes one year, and so did Robert Redford and Art Linkletter. New York Governor Nelson Rockefeller called personally to order several boxes (I remember this because Dad was really excited about it). When Raquel Welch ordered some candy, the boys helping Emil wanted to deliver it in person.

During the Christmas rush they started hiring city firemen to work during their free time to package the candy for mailing. Emil and Mary's son Rick had a friend who worked in the candy mailroom and also worked for the fire department. He suggested his friends come help out, as each year got busier than the previous one. The fire station was close to the business and the men appreciated the extra money at Christmastime.

Through hard work and long hours, Emil and Mary quietly built a successful business that just kept getting both bigger and better. In 1979 their daughter Jamee and her husband Doug joined the business and the list of customers continued to grow. By 1989 mail order customers were approaching 50,000 and Christmas production exceeded 360,000 pounds of toffee.

Enstrom's World Famous Almond Toffee was served on the Captain's table for the final voyage of the Queen Elizabeth. Some was taken twice to Mount Everest climbs thanks to an Enstrom employee connection. The King and Queen of Sweden and other royalty had some for their Christmas.

Dad's retirement idea to have fun making a little bit of candy not only became a big business but also put Grand Junction on the international map.

Land of Opportunity

"Don't just be a taker,
give back to America
whenever you can."
— GUSTAF EMIL ENSTROM

BEFORE MY GRANDFATHER ENSTROM DIED, HE TOLD my father that it was truly a privilege to be able to live in America. He went on to say to Dad, "Don't just be a taker, give back to America whenever you can."

My Grandfather was 19 when he and his parents left Sweden for the United States. Economic conditions in Sweden and several other countries were so bad that many people were migrating to the U.S., "The Land of Opportunity." My father never forgot those words spoken by his father and he truly tried to do his best to give back to his city, county, and state.

Dad was 27 when he, Mother, Emil, and I moved to Grand Junction so Dad could go into the ice cream business with his partner Harry Jones. Dad had not lived in Grand Junction for very many years when he was elected to the City Council in 1935. He served four years including 1939 when he was president of the council (Mayor of Grand Junction). While he was mayor, these are some of the things that were accomplished — the first water purification system installed, an overdue expansion of the sewer system, a street sweeper for the city streets was purchased, and a new, much larger library was built.

Chet and Bus Bergman making toffee for
the Lions Club Carnival, circa 1961

One project done while Dad was on the council could have been generated from selfish desires. Dad loved to play golf and Lincoln Park had a nice golf course but a shack for a clubhouse. The council made a deal with the WPA (the federal Works Progress Administration), which was doing construction in the area at the time, that the city would provide gravel for their construction if they would build a nice clubhouse for the golf course. The deal was signed and the Lincoln Park Golf Course got a nice clubhouse that is still standing.

A smiling Chet Enstrom, third from the left, with fellow El Jebel Shriners

Chet as a 32nd-Degree Mason

Dad served on the Chamber of Commerce Board in 1933 and 1934. He felt that his main contribution to the Chamber was that he convinced the board that North Avenue, which was way north of the city at the time, should be made a by-pass around Grand Junction. He felt that it would eliminate a lot of traffic through Grand Junction that was both unpleasant and an extra expense to the city. Business owners fought it because they thought they would lose business. Finally the business owners were convinced that if tourists wanted to buy something in GJ they would drive into the city to get it. Eventually everyone was happy about it.

Dad and his partner, Harry Jones, decided soon after they went into business that they should join service clubs. Mr. Jones joined Rotary and Dad joined the Lions Club. Dad always supported the club in any way that he could and during his tenure he received many accolades, including Lion of the Year in 1965.

He served as Lions President from 1941 to 1942, but his greatest contribution was a continuing one. He started donating candy for the February Lions Club Carnival in the early 1930s even before he became a Lion. Through the years he and many Lions volunteers made candy, then packed it into boxes donated by Benge's Shoe Store and Brownson's Clothing Store. The boxes had to be cut down by hand to fit the various candy sizes. After the war new boxes were purchased, made especially for Enstrom candies.

A 1959 *Morning Sun* newspaper story told about the Lions Club volunteers and that 400 pounds of Enstrom candies were made for them that year.

Eventually his famous toffee became the big gift, just as it is today. People loved his candy and it brought in a lot of money for the Club's projects, including scholarships to Mesa College. During WWII Dad could barely get enough sugar for his ice cream. Lions Club members donated any extra sugar stamps they could spare so he could continue making the annual Carnival candy.

Dad was a great supporter of Mesa Junior College and later Mesa State College. I am sorry that he didn't live to see it become Colorado Mesa University. He even taught courses in candy making and occasionally he gave lectures at the school on owning a small business.

When Mesa Junior College moved from a one-building structure downtown to a nice new large building on North Avenue at 12th Street, it was within walking distance of our home at 1250 Grand Avenue. After a few years Dad offered to let a financially-struggling student live free in our basement room.

Our basement bedroom was not very luxurious but warm and clean. This was during the worst of the depression and getting to go to college was an extreme luxury. At first girls lived in our basement bedroom, then Dad decided to help football players. He loved football and wanted the Mavericks to have a good team. We had several fine quarterbacks staying in our basement through the years; then WWII started and the football team went to serve its country.

Soon after the war, talk started about making Mesa Junior College a four-year college. Many were for it because of the educational opportunities, others were strongly opposed because it had the reputation of being a prestigious junior college and they were sure it would become a second-rate four-year school. It took nearly 30 years of hard work by a strong committee, including Dad, to finally succeed in completing the groundwork to make it a four-year college. Finally, in 1973 Dad carried the bill to finance it through the State Senate.

Dad remembered the Mason who loaned him money when he was still a youngster, so he joined the Masonic Lodge when he was 22. He was active in the Blue Lodge, then became a 32nd-Degree Mason and a Shriner.

I really do not know how many children Dad helped by getting them to the Shriners' Crippled Children's Hospital. It pained him to see a crippled child and he helped as many as he could. He supported the Masonic projects whole-heartedly. In 1959 he was awarded the 33rd degree for his outstanding work in the Masonic organization and the community. He always considered this his greatest honor. Few are fortunate enough to receive it.

Dad was very patriotic and was disappointed that he was too old to serve in WWII; however, he helped the war effort in many other ways. He was chairman of the gas rationing board, a challenging job. Farmers and some businessmen desperately needed more

Chet and Vernie are on their way to Rome, as Chet was
appointed by President Eisenhower to represent the
United States at the World Dairy Conference.

rationing stamps for gas. One farmer threatened to kill Dad if he didn't get more gas. I am not sure how the problem was solved but Dad survived. Dad participated in fund-raisers and helped the war effort in every way that he could.

He served on the Mesa County United Way board from 1965 through 1971 and was chairman in 1967. He also co-chaired the fund-raising campaign in 1974.

He served on the Mesa County 4-H Council for five years. He was a Director of the Valley Federal Savings and Loan Association for several years and was president of the board for one year.

Dad also served on many other boards: Cystic Fibrosis Association, Colorado-Wyoming Regional Medical Board, the Comprehensive Health Planning Region 7 Board, and the Grand Junction YMCA board. Dad felt it was a real privilege to be able to serve on the Governing Board of Colorado State University. His special responsibility was to oversee Fort Lewis College in Durango, Colorado. At the end of his tenure CSU honored him by presenting him the Lory Award for his service.

For 16 years Dad served as a director of the Colorado Dairy Association and he served two years as president. Then he served six years as a Director of the International Association of Ice Cream Manufacturers. It was during this time that President Eisenhower chose Dad and four other ice cream manufacturers from different parts of the U.S. to represent the United States at the World Dairy Congress in Rome, Italy. Mother got to go with him and they extended the five-day meeting into a nice vacation.

In reading this, I am wondering how Dad managed to do so much volunteer work and why he devoted so much of his time to volunteering.

First of all, I think it was a time when Grand Junction was experiencing dramatic growth and leadership was needed. Dad had the ability to lead and was willing to do it. His dad would have been proud of him because he truly gave back to his city, county, state, and nation.

Senator Enstrom

*"He started the tradition of bringing goodies
to the legislature, which turned
a little old candy shop in
Grand Junction into an economic
force in Mesa County."*
— RICK ENSTROM, GRANDSON

D AD WAS ALWAYS INTERESTED IN POLITICS. His interest probably came from his father, who preached to the family that America and democracy are great and that everyone should appreciate this wonderful country.

Dad registered as a Republican when he was 21. Before many years passed he started attending caucuses and became active in the Republican Party. When we lived at 1250 Grand Avenue in the 30s and 40s, Dad was usually the precinct committeeman. He always had the caucus meetings at our home even though just a few neighbors would attend. Dad tried to explain to people how important it was to attend the caucuses so that they could vote for the person whom they hoped would be the candidate in the coming elections, but still few would attend.

He went on to become more and more active in the party. Eventually, Dad was elected Mesa County Republican Chairman, an office he held for several years. Not only was Dad extremely interested in local and state politics, he followed national politics constantly. One of my happy memories is sitting with Dad by the

State Senator Chet Enstrom

radio listening to the returns being broadcast from the podium at the National Conventions.

In 1966, Senator Ed Lamb resigned to run for another office. Dad was appointed to fill that vacancy. Six months later he was then elected to the Colorado State Senate where he served for eight more years. During his tenure as State Senator he served on the following committees and was chairman of several: Education, Natural Resources, Institutions, Agricultural, Water, Finance, Urban Affairs, and Game Fish and Parks. He was also on the very powerful Appropriations and the Joint Budget Committees. Dad always felt that each committee was extremely important and he tried to make a worthwhile contribution to each one.

He was very proud of the fact that many of the bills and resolutions that he introduced were passed and signed by the Governor. He tried to make some headway on refining the teachers' tenure policy but soon found he could not fight the teachers' union. He felt that his greatest accomplishments as a Senator were the help he gave the committee that was working to make Mesa Junior College a four-year college and the financing he got approved for the post-secondary vocational technical schools (vo-tech schools) in the Delta-Montrose area, Cortez, Boulder, Ft. Collins, and the big Auraria community college in Denver.

Dad wanted every young person to be able to get advanced knowledge or training in his field of interest whether it was a profession or a trade.

For a while after Dad was elected, he had a problem with some of the people in Grand Junction. Because he had been such a strong leader in Grand Junction, many thought Dad could get more for Grand Junction and that Denver should get much less. Dad had not been in the Senate very long when he figured out that Denver and the eastern slope would always get a larger portion of the state money and attention.

As he explained to the Grand Junction residents, there are many more people and problems in eastern Colorado. They have the votes to get the whole amount and the only way to get assets for western Colorado is to cooperate with the representatives from eastern

Colorado. Dad worked very hard to understand the problems of the whole state and in turn they listened to the needs for his district. By cooperating and working together with members of the House as well as his Senate colleagues Dad was able to do a lot for Mesa County and his district.

Dad admired Abraham Lincoln and believed in his political philosophy. Dad told me many times that he always tried to live by Lincoln's philosophy, specifically:

- You cannot bring about prosperity by discouraging thrift.
- You cannot help small men by tearing down big men.
- You cannot strengthen the weak by weakening the strong.
- You cannot help the poor by destroying the rich.
- You cannot lift the wage earner by pulling down the wage payer.
- You cannot further the brotherhood of men by inciting class hatred.

I truly believe that Dad lived by that philosophy and as a result he was able to accomplish a great deal for the district that elected him to the Colorado State Senate.

Backstory Notes
Politics is a complicated business that requires many skills. Drafting bills and getting sponsors to sign on is a start, and once they're introduced they require negotiating skill to get them passed. At times, a bill will wind up being postponed indefinitely by the committee responsible for it. Other bills find momentum and are passed. Once both the House and Senate agree, the final bill is enacted, ready for the Governor's signature.

That tortuous path was taken by Senator Enstrom's bill to convert Mesa Junior College into a four-year school, Mesa State College, and get it funded.

Chet's bill to do that got locked up in committee. The session was ending, but with Chet's agreement Rep. Tillman Bishop got the House to pass a similar bill and send it to the Senate almost immediately. That pried loose the support for Chet's bill and it passed the Senate. The "conformed" bill then went to the Governor, who signed it.

Mesa State College began offering baccalaureate degree programs in 1974, Chet's last year in the Senate.

Representative Bishop ran for the Enstrom Senate seat and handily won. He continued in that role for 24 years.

Among his other community jobs today, he is Chairman of the Legends sculpture project. The sculpture of his old colleague, Chet (and Vernie) Enstrom, is the ninth larger-than-life Legends bronze. The stories told by these sculptures are a "walking tour of history" in Downtown Grand Junction.

Art, Golf, and the Golden Years

"Some people live and die
and never truly live.
Dad lived every minute
of his fruitful life."
— ANN ENSTROM SCOTT

D AD WAS JUST 72 WHEN HE DECIDED THAT eight-and-one-half years in the state Senate were enough, so he declined to run again. He was in good health and very active and he wondered what he would do when he no longer went to Denver. Emil and Mary had the candy business going and growing but Dad knew Emil could use his help during Christmas.

Dad made beautiful Christmas candy canes and many other Christmas candies. He also knew that Emil would need his help during Easter because he also made beautiful candy Easter eggs. But he wondered what he would do the rest of the time.

My husband, Steve, decided to give Dad a "paint by number" picture to paint to see if Dad might have an interest in painting. He had shown some artistic ability when he decorated ice cream specials and when he decorated candy.

It worked! Dad enjoyed painting the picture and then he decided to take some art classes at his favorite college, Mesa State. Soon he was painting a lot of pictures and giving them to anyone who would take them.

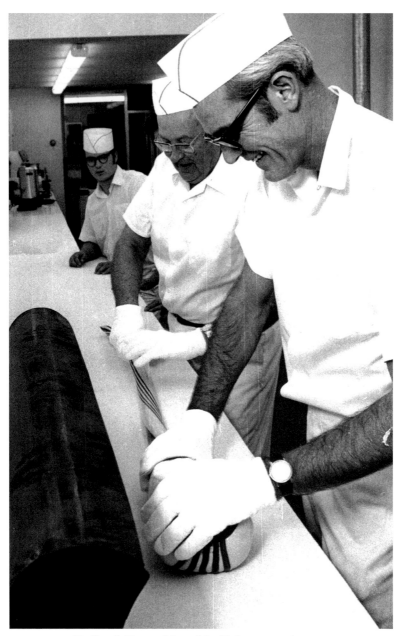

Emil and Chet making a big Christmas candy cane

Chet with some of his paintings

For years he painted the picture the whole family used on our Christmas cards. He spent many enjoyable hours painting in the recreation room at Lakeside where he and Mother lived.

Of course he played a lot of golf at the Bookcliff Country Club, where he was one of the original members. Mother played with him much of the time. They took a walk every day when the weather permitted and they watched all kinds of sports on television. He had time to enjoy the American Lutheran Church and was an active Mason. Dad enjoyed his retirement even though his body had some aches and pains.

Dad played golf with two of his Swedish friends on a Sunday afternoon at the Bookcliff Country Club. He went into St. Mary's Hospital the next day for surgery. He died peacefully ten days later on October 1, 1992. He was 89 years old.

Posthumously, he was inducted into the Colorado Business Hall of Fame in 1994.

Some people live and die and never truly live. Dad lived every minute of his fruitful life.

Vernie and Chet on the golf course

Artist and ex-Senator Enstrom shows his
hand-painted and signed cans. He made these
to celebrate the 1976 Colorado Centennial.

A sunny day in the high country

Skiing
in Western Colorado

*"The Ski Club completed a very successful
and enjoyable year of activity. Among their events
was a delightful overnight skiing trip to
Grand Mesa, where one of the
finest ski courses in the state is situated."*
— GRAND JUNCTION HIGH SCHOOL YEARBOOK 1940

I T WAS 1935 WHEN DAD, A GOOD NORSEMAN, decided that our family should learn to ski. I was ten and Emil was seven. Dad approached Sam Sedalnick, the owner of L. Cooks Sporting Goods, to see if he would be interested in going to Denver to get skies for both families and possibly Sam could start selling ski equipment, if they could work out a deal in Denver.

Dad and Sam drove to Denver and found a manufacturer, the Thor Groswold Ski Company. Dad had known Thor Groswold while in his teens. Thor had come from Norway to start a Colorado ski company because he thought skiing was about to start here. He first landed in Colorado Springs and was looking for someone who could speak his language. He was directed to Dad and they had a short but friendly contact. Thor soon left Colorado Springs for Denver where he became very successful. So Dad and Sam returned home with skis for each family member and a deal for L. Cooks to sell Groswold ski equipment.

**Vernie on a Grand Mesa
picnic table buried in snow**

The skis were long — very long — and bulky with one strap to go over the instep of the foot. For some reason, skiers thought skis had to be very long and unmanageable. Our ski boots were our over-shoes. For clothes we wore wool snow pants, jackets, hats, and gloves. Of course, everything soon became wet and cold but we kept on skiing.

There were two places where a few people were doing a little skiing in 1935. One was near Collbran and the other was on the south side near Cedaredge. Most of those skiing were making their own skis. They would take the narrow boards (skis) and soak the ends of them in water to get them to turn up at the toe. Then they would put some kind of beeswax on them to make them slick. The Enstroms and the Sedalnicks first tried skiing near Cedaredge but it wasn't steep enough to be very interesting.

There was a CCC Camp located on the Land's End road above the Wild Rose Campground on the west side of Grand Mesa. CCC stands for Civilian Conservation Corps, a program started by President Roosevelt during the depths of the depression. It was designed to tackle the problem of unemployed young men between the ages of 18 and 25. It was set up like the Army with officers in charge of the men, who lived in barracks. The pay was $30 a month and $22 of it was sent home to dependents. The boys planted trees, built public parks, built roads and bridges, and a range of other projects that helped to conserve the environment.

Between 1933 and 1941 over 3,000,000 men served in the CCC program across the nation. Dad suggested to the local CCC camp superintendent that he get a few pair of skis so that the boys could have some recreation in the winter. The superintendent went for the suggestion and soon there was a short run and a couple of jumps at the camp. The boys thought it was great fun. Our family and several other families were soon sharing the run with the boys. This lasted a year. There was no tow and the hill was packed by everyone side-stepping from the bottom to the top then going straight down — "schussing." Because the ski run faced south, it wasn't too successful, but Emil and I had a lot of fun while it lasted.

The camp site and ski run are still visible, although now just odd marks, to anyone driving down the Lands End Road.

About 50 people in the area were skiing in 1936. The Grand Junction Winter Sports Club was organized in 1937 to get skiing going on Grand Mesa. Dad was either the first or second president of the club. Mesa Lakes Resort was chosen as the area to develop into a ski area. The membership in the club grew to 150 people the next year and the members worked hard to develop the quarter-mile run, which started on the hill in front of the resort and ended on Beaver Lake. There was a three-sided shelter next to the course where a fire was kept burning to warm the skiers.

After a while a rope tow was installed. The Lions' club gave the Ski Club $50 to purchase the rope. A four-cylinder Ford Model T engine mounted on a chassis provided the power to pull the skiers up the hill. This tow lasted for about three years with a lot of effort from the Ski Club members. There is an old picture of one member in a tree hoisting up the motor with a bear at the bottom of the tree looking up. The bear had come to investigate but wasn't too interested and sauntered away, but it gave those present a little scare.

A morning ritual on the days that the course was open was for two men to side step up the ski course with two charged batteries. It was their hope that the batteries would start the motor to pull the rope tow. To pack the course everyone had to side step to the top. It was mandatory that when one fell, he had to fill his hole (sitzmark) and pack it down for the safety of the other skiers.

The rope tow was a great invention but the rope would get wet and icy. Our hands would slip and we couldn't hang on. Someone came up with a clamp which would go over the rope then one would hang onto the clamp with both hands. It wasn't too successful either. It took several good mechanics to keep the motor running to keep the tow pulling the skiers up the hill.

We seldom knew for sure if the highway department would clear the road to the resort. We would call Cooks on Sunday mornings to find out if the road would be open. When they did plow the road, it was only plowed to a dead end with only a little space for extra parking. Often there was no space for cars to turn around when it was time to come home. Sometimes eight or ten men would surround a car and would bounce it up and down turning it a bit each time until it was headed home. After a few cars had left, the rest could manage to turn around. Of course everyone had to put chains on the back wheels, which was not a fun task. In spite of these little problems, we had a wonderful time skiing.

Skiing grew! By 1939 the Grand Junction High School had a ski club and many students were into skiing. In the 1940 Yearbook it said, "The Ski Club completed a very successful and enjoyable year of activity. Among their events was a delightful overnight skiing trip to Grand Mesa where one of the finest ski courses in the state is situated." (I think that statement was a little biased, but there were very few ski courses in Colorado at that time.) We stayed in cabins with wood stoves and outdoor plumbing but we girls had a great time skiing with our boyfriends in the moonlight over the frozen, snow-covered lakes. In 1941 the high school yearbook said that the dues were raised to 75 cents so that the club could send two members to race at Estes Park. The country was still in a depression and 75 cents was not always easy to get. A decent pair of skis cost about $12 and few could afford that.

Skiing was curtailed in 1942 due to the gas rationing. It was not patriotic to use gas to go skiing, even if you happened to have a little

Winter transportation for Grand Mesa

Chet, Vernie, Ann, and a friend,
Dorothy Bruce, on Grand Mesa

extra gas. The GJ Ski Club invested its money in war bonds for use after the war. Membership in the club was $1 at that time.

Every spring while I was in junior high and high school, the family would go to Aspen at least once to ski. There was only one run, which is more or less where Ajax Ski run is now. It was a long run. At the bottom of the run was a rope tow that would take one up about a quarter of the way. Then the next tow that would take one up another third of the way was made up of two flat-bottom boats. A cable would pull the boats up and down. We would take our skis off and put them in the bottom of the boat or on a rack in the back of the boat. Then we would sit on the sides of the boat. The last trek to the top of the run was very steep and one had to side step to get there. The top part was called the "Corkscrew" and it was a difficult and challenging run.

I don't remember ever skiing the Corkscrew but going up to where the boat tow stopped and skiing down from there was enough of a thrill for me. Skiing at Aspen was great, especially in the spring. Staying at the Hotel Jerome cost $2.50 a night for our family. Dinners were $1.50, and lunches and breakfasts were 25 to 50 cents. For a dollar one could ride all day on the "boat tow" and the rope tow.

After the war a new site was chosen for a ski area on Grand Mesa. A new road leading toward the top of Grand Mesa went right through our ski course. The new location was lower down the mountain and along Mesa Creek. It was better because being lower, the state highway department could keep the road open more easily. Grand Junction Ski Club went to work to make a very good ski area and it was used until Powderhorn was finished in 1966.

Volunteers worked all summer to clear and prepare the Mesa Creek Ski course for winter skiing. Sam Sedalnick donated a rope and the ski club bought a rope for the rope tows. A Ford Model A motor ran the shorter tow and a Buick hearse engine operated the longer tow. Both motors were placed at the top of the tows and big drums of gasoline had to be hauled up the hill to them.

The ski club continually had financial problems but eventually enough people skied that they had come to believe that skiing was a part of Grand Junction life. They invested in the club and it was finally on its way. In 1960 they were able to add a Poma lift that was wonderful for the skiers.

When we first started skiing, all we knew to do was to go straight down the hill and hope for the best. This "method" continued until a doctor and his wife moved to Grand Junction from Austria to escape Hitler and the Nazi regime. They had skied a lot in Europe and were beautiful skiers. They knew how to ski under control, how to stop and to turn. They immediately tried to teach everyone how to "snowplough," probably for their own safety. There were probably more snowploughers on Grand Mesa than any place in the world. The boys were not sold on the idea of skiing under control but we girls and the older people thought it was a good idea. We all eventually learned to control our skis and a lot of good skiers came out of Grand Mesa skiing.

When I went to college in Colorado Springs, I would ski at Glen Cove on Pikes Peak. Occasionally, I would ride with Bud Maytag (Maytag washing machine family). He seemed to have gas because each car was allotted so much gas during the war. Having money has always been such a convenience! Once in a while we girls would ride the train to Winter Park to ski but it was not easy to make arrangements because the trains were used to transport soldiers.

Some of my friends and I dated Tenth Mountain Division boys from Camp Hale near Leadville and they could get gas to drive to Glen Cove. They were excellent skiers and fine young men. One spring when my friend Jane came to Grand Junction with me for spring break, we met the boys we were dating from Camp Hale in Aspen for a couple days of skiing — chaperoned by my parents, of course — but we had fun. Far too many of those fine young men were killed in the invasion of northern Italy in spite of their excellent condition and training. It was a great tragedy. I didn't ski again on Grand Mesa until the children and I moved back to Grand Junction in 1963 after I was divorced. My folks thought it would be nice for the children to learn to ski as a new experience after living in Phoenix for several years. They bought us a family membership and let us use their four-wheel-drive car. Then Mother would have dinner ready for us when we got home. What great grandparents the children had! Our sons Chet and Lee had tried skiing a little in Salt Lake when we lived there but they didn't take to it too much. It was so cold and they were pretty young but now they were ready to go.

At first our son John did not like it. He couldn't master it the first day and he was mad and discouraged. On the way home he said, "I am not going to ski again until I am 33." I told him that was fine and he could stay home with Grammy and Granddad the next Sunday. But by the next Sunday he was ready to try it again and things went much better. He was soon skiing right along with Chet and Lee. They all grew to love skiing. I skied when I could but often I sat in the car and graded papers.

After Steve and I were married, the family skied at Stoner, near Cortez. We also skied at Purgatory near Durango. Steve had never skied before we were married but he was a very good sport and gave it the old college try. When we moved to Montrose, we skied at Telluride, Dallas Divide, and Monarch Pass and we did have fun. Steve got to where he enjoyed it somewhat but he was not disappointed when I decided at 55 to give it up while my bones were all still intact.

The Powderhorn Ski Area was opened officially in a big dedication ceremony on December 5, 1966. Fifteen hundred people attended the dedication to see Governor John Love cut the ribbon. My Dad was so pleased to be there to see the dedication and to realize how skiing had progressed since he and Sam went to Denver to get skis almost 30 years earlier. In spite of the wonderful tows, beautiful runs, and lovely resort, I wonder if the skiers today have more fun than we did skiing out of control and hoping for a happy landing.

Backstory Notes
When Chet Enstrom chatted with young Thor Groswold in 1923 he probably encouraged the young Norwegian to continue pursuing his dream: bringing his homeland's national sport to America. Groswold succeeded in both making skis and in bringing the sport to his new country.

Skis made by his Groswold Ski Company were exceptional and were used in Olympic competition. Gretchen Fraser skied on Groswold skis in 1948, winning America's first Olympic Alpine Skiing Gold Medal in Slalom in St. Moritz.

Thor Groswold succeeded in his impossible dream, making his wooden skis and also spreading the word to make skiing a popular winter sport in America. His accomplishments are recognized by his selection to the National and Colorado Ski Halls of Fame. His sport grew steadily and his company did too. It thrived from the early 1920s until it finally closed in 1952 for personal reasons. His legacy can be seen today in any of the winter snow states. There are now too many ski courses to count and the winter sports business is huge, with no end in sight.

The only poster ever produced for the Groswold Ski Company shows the company's brand, ski jumpers.

A Groswold Ski leans against the company truck window.

Vernie Elizabeth (Morgan) Enstrom

*"Mr. Speaker, it is my privilege to pay tribute to
Vernie E. Enstrom for the great strides she took in
establishing herself as a valuable leader in the Grand Junction
community. Her dedication to family, friends, work,
and the community certainly deserve the recognition
of this body of Congress and a grateful nation."*
— SCOTT MCINNIS

MY MOTHER HAD A BEAUTIFUL LIFE. THERE WERE a few valleys but mostly her life was filled with beautiful mountains.

She was born October 22, 1904 a few minutes after her twin, John Virgil, had come into this world. Her birth took place in her parents' home on a farm near Atwood, Kansas. She was the last-born of her parents' 11 children. People have told me that Mother was a happy, pretty young lady with dark wavy hair, brown eyes, and long black eyelashes

My mother's parents, Leander Lee and Anna Elizabeth Morgan, moved from Red Oak, Iowa to Northwestern Kansas a few years after they were married. They eventually acquired enough land to make a success of mostly wheat farming. This is where my mother grew up, and the farm, which was always dear to her, is still in the hands of descendents of L. L. and Anna Morgan.

Mother had three sisters and seven brothers. Five of the boys were between Mother and her next sister so she grew up playing

Vernie in Kansas at about age 16   **Vernie in Kansas at about age 19**

with boys instead of dolls. She loved all the farm animals and helped care for many of them.

Music was a big part of Mother's life. She started singing as a child and continued singing until she could sing no more. She was still able to sing her great grandchildren to sleep. Most of the Morgan family was very musical. Mother's dad played the fiddle. He was playing in some kind of a musical group when he met my grandmother. The group was playing for a dance and when Grandfather saw her dance by, he knew he wanted to get to know her. He did get to know her and a year or so later, they were married. Granddad continued playing the fiddle after the family moved to Kansas and he even gave some of the neighboring children violin lessons.

The home was filled with music. Mother sang alto, played the piano by ear or by note, and she played the banjo and guitar. In high school Mother had a lot of fun playing the banjo in a quartet.

Grandmother wanted Mother and her twin brother, Virg, to get at least one year of high school in Colorado Springs where she thought they would get a better education. As I understand it, from reading letters and hearing things my mother told me through the years, my grandmother Morgan did not dislike Kansas but she liked Red Oak, Iowa and Colorado Springs better. Her family in Iowa was prosperous. Her father was a successful farmer and life had been quite a bit easier there than homesteading in Kansas. I think that is why she wanted something better for her last daughter and son.

So she found a house to rent in Colorado Springs and the twins graduated from Colorado Springs High School. After graduation Mother went another year for a post high school course where she learned how to cook, sew, and become a homemaker. I never heard Mother mention that she might have liked to stay in Kansas for her

A quiet day on the lake

Chauffeur-driven around the course

senior year. She did many times mention that she loved Kansas and told me often how beautiful the mature wheat was when the wind blew, making the wheat look like a waving ocean of gold. She eventually fell in love with Colorado Springs too.

A little more than a year after Mother finished her post high school course, she and my father were married in Castle Rock, Colorado on May 19, 1924.

Mother was the perfect wife for Dad. She supported him completely in everything he ever wanted to do. She was always there for him.

Mother was a very happy young wife. She lived in Colorado Springs surrounded by some of her family members and all of Dad's family members. She had a three-year-old daughter and a nine-month-old son, and she had recently moved into a nice home that Dad had helped build for her. In addition, Dad had a good job in an upscale confectionary. What more could a young, 25-year-old wife want?

I am sure she was shocked when Dad came home late in 1928 and told her he had a great opportunity to move to Grand Junction and go into the ice cream business with a partner she had hardly met. Mother and Dad had saved about a thousand dollars, which in those days was a lot of money, and that was Dad's contribution to the partnership.

Dad's partner, Harry Jones, had inherited some money, so between them they had the money to buy a struggling dairy business and it was Mother's job to move herself and her two children to Grand Junction. She was leaving her secure surroundings to go where she knew no one and had no idea what to expect.

I am sure that Mother shed many tears before she got on the train with her babies, but she was willing to go and I doubt that she complained much to my Dad. That wasn't her nature.

The move to Grand Junction was not simple. Harry Jones had already moved to town the summer of 1928 to get the business started. Dad had gone before Mother, arriving on March 3, 1929 after a two-day trip. He rode with a dairy equipment salesman who wanted the new Jones-Enstrom venture to be a customer. The two new partners bought some of the salesman's equipment and on March 4 Velvet Ice Cream was born.

After packing up the Colorado Springs house and saying goodbye to friends and family, Mother, Emil, and I came to the new town by train.

It wasn't an easy adjustment because at first we all lived upstairs in a small apartment over the dairy. This created a difficult situation — no conveniences, cramped and lonely. Eventually Dad found an apartment not far from the business and things started to improve. A few years later Dad was able to buy the house at 1250 Grand Avenue, where they lived for more than 30 years.

When Mother got to Grand Junction she immediately started going to the First Christian Church where she made lifelong friends. Emil and I got to go along because there was no one to take care of us. Dad and Mr. Jones took turns working on Sundays and the Sunday when each was off, he would head for the golf course; they both loved to play golf.

Mother learned to play bridge so she could socialize with the ladies in Grand Junction and soon belonged to a bridge club. When Emil and I were in grade school, Mother would go to the library and check out three or four books and would read them all in a week. One day Mother said, "I am being selfish spending so much time reading just for my pleasure. I need to be doing something to help others part of my time." She continued reading but not nearly as much.

Chet and Vernie celebrate 25 years
in the ice cream business, 1954.

She became active in the P.T.A. at Lincoln School and she assumed other volunteer jobs. Mother and Mrs. Clyde Biggs started the Girl Scouts in Grand Junction when Betsy Biggs Zollner and I were in the fifth grade. Mother always attended any activity in which either Emil or I was involved.

She learned to ski because Dad wanted all of us to ski together before there was really any skiing in the area. She hated the cold but she would don her skis and do her best to make several runs down the easy slope. She was always relieved to get home without a broken limb.

Dad loved to fish so in the early 40s Mother and Dad bought a cabin on Sunset Lake on Grand Mesa, which they enjoyed for about 20 years. Mother learned to fly fish and became one of the best fly fisherwomen on Grand Mesa. She fooled hundreds of fish with her delicate casting touch. Mother was always a gracious hostess to all of the friends whom Dad invited to spend a day or a weekend. She particularly enjoyed having the grandchildren spend time at the cabin.

Mother learned to play golf because Dad enjoyed it. She started playing when the golf course at the Bookcliff Country Club opened and when Dad finally retired from most of his projects they played a lot of golf together. Mother got to be a pretty good golfer and truly enjoyed it. She even hit a hole in one!

She wasn't particularly happy when Dad agreed to manage the Bookcliff Country Club in 1961 while it was between managers. It was to be for a very short time, just until the board could find a new manager. Since Dad had sold the ice cream business and the candy business was just starting, he had the time to help out for a short time. As the "short time" went on for many months, Mother got tired of having Dad gone so much and she was very tired of running the candy kitchen mostly by herself. She was very happy when the board hired a permanent manager.

When Dad decided to pursue his candy-making hobby, Mother was his right-hand lady. Dad might never have come up with his toffee recipe if he had not had Mother's help and support. For years she would reach into the boiling pot of candy with a long-handled spoon and quickly pull out an almond and douse it into cold water, bite into the nut, and if the nut was cooked she would tell Dad that the candy was ready to pour onto the water-cooled table. She also helped in many other ways. When they started their little business, Mother learned to pack the toffee, take orders, wait on customers, all while helping to make candy. Then, of course, she got to do most of the clean-up.

She joined the Soroptimist women's organization when she became involved in Dad's business. One year she was honored as the Soroptimist of the Year and a year later the Lions Club honored her as the Lioness of the Year.

When Dad decided to go into politics, Mother was willing to sell her home at 1250 Grand Avenue, move into a condo at Lakeside, and then make another home in an apartment in Denver. I never heard her complain about keeping up two places then flying back and forth every weekend while the legislature was in session. She attended most of the Senate sessions and felt at ease with prominent politicians. She became involved in the Republican party of Grand Junction and helped in any way that she could. Dad called her his "First Lady."

Mother had truly had a beautiful life by the time she died on March 20, 2002, at the age of 97. Colorado Representative Scott McInnis paid tribute to Mother in the U.S. House of Representatives a few days after she died. He concluded:

> "Mr. Speaker, it is my privilege to pay tribute to Vernie E. Enstrom for the great strides she took in establishing herself as a valuable leader in the Grand Junction community. Her dedication to family, friends, work, and the community certainly deserve the recognition of this body of Congress and a grateful nation. Although Vernie has left us, her good-natured spirit lives on through the lives of those she touched. I would like to extend my regrets and deepest sympathies to Vernie's family and friends during their time of bereavement and remembrance. She was a remarkable woman and she will be greatly missed."

Taming Times
and Temperatures

EVER WONDER WHEN YOU WERE CRUNCHING DOWN on a bite of that unbelievably delicious Enstrom almond toffee how it came about?

Ann Enstrom Scott's memories in this book give you the big story, but of course there are many more intriguing little details.

It seems ironic today that Chet Enstrom's first toffee in Grand Junction was just for a special ice cream flavor, Butter Brickle. Back then he was all-in in the ice cream business. Special flavors were being developed all across America to spur sales. Because he was a master of both candy and ice cream, Chet developed many unique and original "flavor of the month" tastes for Velvet Ice Cream.

When the ice cream business was solidly on its feet Chet could devote some time to his other love, making candies of all kinds.

He started learning the ice cream business at Barthel's Confectionary in Colorado Springs (an elite and popular place) when he was 18 years old. Chet improved the ice cream so much and worked so well he became manager of that process.

Ice cream sales were slow in the winter so Chet also volunteered to help the candy maker. In those days candy recipes were jealously-guarded secrets, but while washing pots and pans in the candy shop he watched the candy maker closely. He started a recipes "diary" of the many candies he watched being made. The candy maker left for another job and Chet took over, making candy and supervising the ice cream plant too.

The recipes he wrote down starting in 1922, along with many others he developed, became "Chet's Little Black Book." It came to Grand Junction with him and is still in use at Enstrom Candies today.

The Barthel's Confectionary soda shop,
with a fountain, ice cream, and shelves
full of candies made on the premises,
is where Chet Enstrom started working
when he was 18 years old, and where he
learned a great deal about making both
ice cream and candy.

Chet is shown with his early model timer open. The wheels inside trigger the correct light bulb to turn off after the right amount of cooking time.

In the 1930s Chet was making more candies of every kind each year. In about 1954 he and Vernie turned it into a small business, and rented a place across the alley from the ice cream plant for their candy project. They were also making more and better almond toffee each year.

Of all the delicious recipes in that treasured "Black Book," one turned into a precious jewel. It was that "Butter Brickle" flavor. Experiments off and on through the years led to a consistent product. It was "perfect" by 1954, destined to become Chet's World Famous Almond Toffee. That original recipe, using all natural and

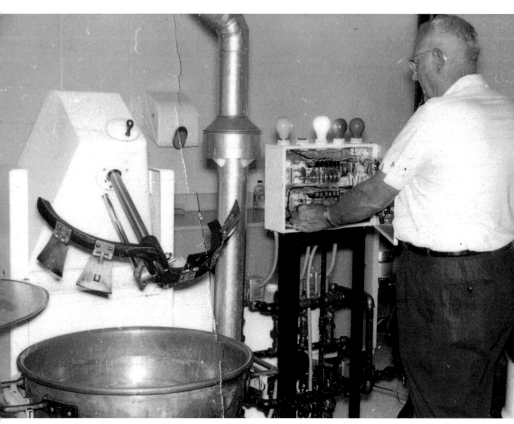

Accurately timing how long each
part of the mix cooks, and at what
temperature, is a critical part of
Chet's World Famous Almond Toffee.
This later model of his timer ran
the automated mixer and turned the
heat on and off for perfect mixing
temperatures.

fresh ingredients, is still in use today along with the same attention to the tricky details of making every delicious bite exactly right.

Getting each batch of toffee to be uniformly good was a series of connected problems. What if each batch was different? Some to Chet's high standard, others not. Why did one batch taste wonderful, another like it was scorched? Why did the butter in a batch separate out?

He and Vernie made lots of almond toffee using their skills and experience over the years. By trial and error they mastered the variables. They couldn't make any of their candy full-time because making rich, high-quality Velvet Ice Cream was the main job.

In 1954 their candy sales were modest: $911.70 total that year. They did a whopping $1,174 in 1955.

The candy business grew from that modest start. Chet knew he had to do more than heat his copper pot over an open flame, stir with a wooden pick handle, and then pour it out on the marble cooling slab. He bought these tools for $85 from a former candy maker in Montrose.

Batch after batch, Chet stirred and added the various parts like butter and almonds. Vernie jotted down the time and heat for each part of every batch. There were an amazing number of variables. Stir too fast and the butter would whip out of the mix. Too much heat with the almonds and the toffee tasted scorched. Too little heat and the ingredients would separate.

Vernie was a talented musician, so what would be more fitting than to set those cooking times to music? It worked pretty well. Except that the demand for almond toffee kept growing and at times Vernie wasn't available to sing.

Chet was, among other attributes, a skilled tinkerer. That led to an electric timer he developed so other workers could follow the demanding toffee cooking and mixing timetable.

Chet's timer with its four light bulbs on top was a major innovation. The butter and sugar had to reach a certain heat and mix time. The almonds had to cook exactly the right time for maximum flavor. Vernie had the job of tasting a cooked almond (after cooling it) to verify that each batch had that perfect almond flavor.

Those years of experiments and tweaking had the times and temperatures exactly right, so Chet's newly devised electric box cued the time for each stage. The four light bulbs on top would be on to start, and as each stage ended a bulb would turn off.

The end result was a no-more-guesswork almond toffee. Every batch was, predictably, made to Chet's delicious toffee standard: uniformly good. And it let them work through eight batches totaling 224 pounds every day. Every 10 days they could produce a ton of almond toffee. The mom and pop candy hobby started to grow into a full-fledged business.

Today that business is 55 years old. Enstrom Candies with Chet's World Famous Almond Toffee is a huge business that keeps getting even bigger. Today's building at 701 Colorado Avenue is too small and will have to be expanded.

At some point it's likely the fourth Enstrom generation will be running this amazing family business, building further on the successful lessons learned, year by year, of their great grandparents, their grandparents, and of course Mom and Dad.

You can bet they'll still follow that simple little Enstrom rule: make some good candy for friends and family. All those friends are almost family anyway and they're now all over the world.

— KEN JOHNSON
Legends of the Grand Valley
September 26, 2014

ABOUT THE AUTHORS

Ann Enstrom Scott

Ann Enstrom Scott wrote this book over several years from "bits and pieces" of her family memories; memories to preserve and share with her children and grandchildren.

Ann's insights engage us in the lives of her parents, Chet and Vernie Enstrom, and the intriguing history of what is now an 85-year-old family business. They relate how the Enstrom Candies of today came to be, including the long path to perfect the significant World Famous Almond Toffee.

These stories reveal the Enstrom's life and work in Grand Junction, generous contributions to the community, and how they helped skiing get its start in the Grand Valley. All those years they overcame changing business patterns and changing times. Enstrom Candies, Inc., with customers all over the world, is now owned by the third Enstrom generation, with the fourth one in the wings. Ann and her husband Steve live in Windsor, Colorado.

Ken Johnson

Ken Johnson, Grand Junction native, is an author and newspaperman who has owned, published, and edited 17 newspapers from California to Florida, from Grand Junction to Cleveland, Ohio.

He has developed and published national magazines, been a graphic arts consultant and has researched and written books about Grand Junction and Western Colorado history.

He was owner, publisher, and editor of *The Daily Sentinel* and a founding partner of the *Grand Junction Free Press*.

Since 2003 he has been active in the development and success of the Legends of the Grand Valley's Historic Story Sculptures program. These larger-than-life sculptures create a "Walking Tour of History" throughout downtown Grand Junction.

Legends Chairman
Tillie Bishop with
co-chairs
Miffie Blozvich and
Jacquie Chappell-Reid

It started in 2003. The goal of the Legends Historic Sculptures Project is to preserve and showcase stories of historically significant men and women who shaped our community. Long-dead visionaries were being forgotten, yet they were the foundation builders for all the good things we share today in this unique place we call home.

The Legends group commissions a larger-than-life bronze of a "local legend" each year. The sculptures tell the stories of these amazing citizens who were successful in business, in the business of living, and in the business of helping to build — and grow — a thriving community.

Miffie Blozvich and Jacquie Chappell-Reid helped to lead the reprinting of Dalton Trumbo's scandalous 1935 novel Eclipse, based on life in Grand Junction, which raised over $65,000 for the Library Foundation. That led to the 2007 bronze of Grand Junction High School graduate Trumbo, the guy in the bathtub writing a movie script, maybe a spectacle like "Spartacus" or "Exodus."

Tilman "Tillie" Bishop, leader of the project, dubbed the group "The Dalton Gang." At the same time, the City of Grand Junction, led by Mayor Bruce Hill, commissioned the George A. Crawford sculpture in time for the city's 125th Anniversary celebration.

With the successful community embrace of the Trumbo project, the committee decided to commemorate five key legends of the Grand Valley: one sculpture a year for five years. The fifth was unveiled September 7, 2012, as part of the Operation Foresight 50th Anniversary celebration. The successful Legends Sculpture Project has continued with two additional sculptures: Prinster and Enstrom and is now into its seventh year.

Together, the sculptures add a historic element to the world-renowned Art on the Corner program in downtown Grand Junction. Community partners in the Legends project include the City of Grand Junction, Downtown Development Authority, Museum of Western Colorado, Western Colorado Center for the Arts, and Colorado Mesa University.

Anyone interested in this ongoing gift to the community is welcome to join the committee. Contributions are welcomed and encouraged.

Please contact a Legends leader for more information
Tillie Bishop, Chairman 970.242.9230
Jacquie Chappell-Reid Co-Chair, 970.640.5350
Miffie Blozvich, Co-Chair 970.260.8130

Mail donations to
Legends Sculpture Project
Art on Corner/Legends
c/o Downtown Development Authority
248 South 4th Street
Grand Junction, CO 81501

Karen Jobe Templeton and
Jamee Simons (Enstrom
Candies) across from the
Avalon, at the location for
the Enstrom sculpture

Chet and Vernie Enstrom, in
miniature form, at Seventh and
Main for the sculpture location
selection in early July

Karen Jobe Templeton

Award-winning sculptor Karen Jobe
Templeton specializes in portraiture,
bas relief, and monumental sculpture of
adults, children, and animals. She has
also created several series of realistic and
representational figure sculptures, and steel
and glass sculptures based on petroglyphs of
the prehistoric peoples of North America.

Following 17 years in the health care
profession, Karen left nursing to pursue her
true passion — sculpting. Nursing, often
dealing with people in the most intense hour
of their need, gave her an ability to "see"
people in a way that would vitally impact
her work as a portrait and figure sculptor.

Karen's sculptures are in private
and public collections from the U.S. to
Japan to Bulgaria, including Grand
Junction's Art on the Corner exhibit.
She lives in Helper, Utah.

HISTORIC SCULPTURES

egends

of the Grand Valley

Support for the
Story Sculpture Project

Thank you for supporting this important community project. Your participation helps to preserve and showcase for posterity the stories of the innovative men and women who have contributed so much to our sense of place in the Grand Valley.

Yes, I would like to participate in this project as a Legends supporter.

PLEASE ACCEPT MY GIFT OF

☐ $25   ☐ $50   ☐ $75   ☐ $100   ☐ $150   ☐ $200   ☐ $500   ☐ $750   ☐ Other $_____

Check enclosed $_____

Please charge my credit card $_____   ☐ Visa   ☐ MC

Account # _____   Exp_____/_____

Signature _____

Name _____

Mailing Address _____

City/State/Zip _____

Phone_____ Email _____

Please make your contribution **payable to** Art on the Corner Legends
Send to

    Legends of the Grand Valley
    c/o Downtown Development Authority
    248 S. 4th Street
    Grand Junction, CO 81501

Contributions for this project qualify for standard federal and state tax deductions and my also qualify for the Enterprise Zone Tax Credit with a minimum contribution of $50. Contact your accountant for more details.

        Tilman "Tillie" Bishop, Chair 970.242.9230
        Jacquie Chappell-Reid, Co-Chair 970.640.5350
        Miffie Blozvich, Co-Chair 970.260.8130